In the name of God, Most Gracious Most Merciful

Love, Hate and A Bench

By Hüseyin Abudharr Ali-Diakides

Iqra Publishing ©

Contents

Introduction

All praise is due to God
Lord of all that exists,
The answer to every question
At the end of every wish,
The One and Only
The only thing that is,
The only judge who can sentence
Eternal bliss.

All hope lies with God
With Him by your side
You can defeat an Empire
Whilst He makes the sea divide[1]
He can cool the flames
If you're thrown in the fire[2]
He can kiss your heart
And become your one desire,

He can make a new born baby
Speak from the cradle,[3]
Then return millennia later
On the backs of angels[4]
If you need saving
Know that He can save you,

---

[1] Surah ad-Dukhan 44:24

[2] Surah al-Anbiya 21:69

[3] Surah al-Maryam 19:29

[4] Sahih Muslim 7015

You never know the heights
That He can take you

If you're stuck in the desert
He can cause a stream to flow from a stone[5]
He can give a king the power over jinnis
So he can transport a throne[6]
He can build a magical fetus
Within a blessed virgins' womb[7]
And then return him to us
At the very point of our doom[8]

And when you feel
Like the World is against you,
He can send down to earth
An army of angels
All marching in rows[9]
To turn the tables,
You are a miracle,
Don't ever doubt the One who made you

His blessings are infinite
How can I count them?
His miracles are all around us
How can you doubt them?

---

[5] Sahih Bukhari 3364

[6] Surah al-Naml 27:28-30

[7] Surah al-Imran 3:49

[8] Sahih al-Bukhari, Volume 3, Book 43: *Kitab-ul-`Ilm* (Book of Knowledge), Hâdith Number 656

[9] Surah al-Anfal 8:9

He gave us sorrows as strength
How can you drown them?
He gave us our goals and ambitions
Through the path that we found them.

All praise is due to God
Such delicate designs He has written
Like the atmosphere
And the eco-system
And everything submits
To His every command
Except man who tries to resist
The Best of Planner's[10] plan

He made all that exists
In balance like a machine,
And He gave us our role in this tapestry
His merciful deen[11]
Some say we are dreaming
Believing in Him the unseen
Even though all of existence
Is but His dream

Peace exists through submission
To the only thing that truly exists
And you'll search to the stars
When your heart receives His kiss
And awakens His memory
From a time before you were born then

---

[10] Surah al-Imran 3:54

[11] The way of life Muslims must adopt to comply with divine law, encompassing beliefs, character and deeds

Like a dream you can't remember
Just the feelings you had but not what caused them

So Love Him!
Your eternal friend
If you take one step towards Him
He will take ten[12]
Love Him and His love
Will never end
Know there is no break,
That He can't mend

And to love Him
You must love His creation
This beautiful life,
That you've been placed in,
Every day that you exist
Is absolutely amazing
All praise is due to God
So, praise Him

[12] Hadith Qudsi

Part 1

20 Poems of Love & Hate

Foreword

In the name of God, Most Gracious, Most Merciful, Lord of all that exists.

These twenty poems of mine were selected by many friends and have been written over a period of around ten years. They all relate to love or hatred whether that is with God, earthly relationships or friendships. I wanted to show the effects of hatred, whilst exploring the idea of love. All these poems meant something at the time they were written and most of them were written for people in particular, being written for eight different people.

Whilst one of these poems was in fact written in anger and I even changed my view on the situation, I felt it relevant as it showed the anger that I was feeling at the time.

The last of the twenty poems in this collection was written for a man who was like my uncle, Sam Sterling. It's important to understand that although his passing was sad, it was worth celebrating his life as he had a long and substantial one.

I have included footnotes in order to translate some of the Arabic words, which are regularly used within Islam, even when speaking in other languages. This is because I wrote the poems as I would think them and did not take into account how any readers, particularly non-Muslim readers, would understand them. I have also at points used the footnotes to show where I reference the Qur'an or hadeeth.

May God make these poems a force of good and hopefully, should He will it, influence someone.

Poetry

My brain sends signals to my mouth,
And causes me to speak and shout,
But my heart can only speak in rhyme,
Often in conflict with my mind,

Sometimes I'm speechless and stay quiet,
But my pen continues to write,
When it seems I've given up on life,
My poetry continues the fight,

My brain can cause me to stutter and stammer,
But my heart speaks with perfect grammar,
My tongue may seem unforgiving,
But my heart beats to a merciful rhythm,

You can write an entire book back to back,
Filled with many figures, stories and facts,
But you can evoke emotions so strong,
Using a single line of poetry or song.

I Miss You

I miss you,
I believe you miss me as well,
And even though I want you back,
It's a secret I won't tell.

I love you,
Still after all this time,
And even though it's killing me,
If you ask me then I'll say I'm fine.

I need you,
But I must hide my affection,
When I had you I dwelled on your faults,
Now I only remember your perfections.

I want you,
But I haven't even tried,
And though the longing is so strong,
It still can't defeat my pride.

Greed

You sold your soul,
Became a souless soul,
In your heart,
There's an unholy hole,

You have more wealth and power,
Than most will ever know,
But all you can do with it,
Is make it grow,

The path of greed,
Is the path you chose
You're the slug,
That ate the rose,

You're a slave to the lust,
That Shaytan imposed,
But however much you try drink it dry,
The Nile still flows,

What we call misery and death,
You call profit,
To look in your eyes,
There's nothing but greed within those sockets,

What an endless oblivion,
Must be your pockets,
Even your words,
Are nothing but toxic,

Does your heart not beat blood,
Like the blood you spill,

Are you not human,
Like those you kill,

Is there any point trying to reach you,
Knowing you'll do it still,
And even if you stopped following your quest,
Someone else will.

Respect Her

She seemed so sweet when I met her
Beautiful smile, but under it I saw depression,
And her mood could change like London weather,
The other girls diss her cos they don't get her,

But girls out here can be savage,
Did it never occur to you that she's been through
madness?
Hearing her life story is just tragic,
And the fact she came this far to me is magic.

I respect her so much even though she seems so lost,
It's a cold world out here like snow and frost,
People like to chat behind backs about each other,
Smile in her face, but hate on the undercover,

They don't understand her and are jealous,
Of her looks and talent, they don't see her endeavor,
And try to pick on her however,
She continues to stay strong, you don't how much I
respect her.

A World Apart

Listen to the ocean as it breathes so calmly,
Inhale, exhale, inhale, exhale, inhale, exhale,
Never holding its breath,
But it'll breath more aggressive when its angered.
It is sour because its heart has been broken,
Into many seas divided by continents,
Beneath its depths there are so many secrets,
Only Musa could make him open up.

Look to the clouds as they weep,
Pitter patter, pitter patter, pitter patter,
They cry out with a roar that shakes the sky,
And strike out at the world with a piercing light,
They release emotion that have been building for time,
And the world turns darker than coal,
Their pain is so much that they must turn cold,
And freeze the teardrops into snow.

The sun shines it radiance on all that dare to look,
But underneath its smile are hidden tears,
Tears for its curse to never see its true love,
For she is always at the other side of the world.
His lover can only come out at night,
And the sun is destined to create day,
So at dusk and dawn he always hopes,
To catch a glimpse of what he never will.

The wind whispers like a jinni,
Invisible yet it can push you which way it wills,
Sometimes it can send you left sometimes right,

Listen to him at your own risk.
It can make the ocean angry or make him calm,
It can push the clouds where to go,
But he can never push the sun across the globe,
To see the one for who he longs.

The Truth

Sometimes you can seem so narrowminded,

It's like you close your eyes to remain blinded,

And if I didn't care about you then I would remain silent,

But I know the truth and you can find it.

So find it before your soul is taken by Azrayil[13],

I have to believe your heart has no seal,

I can't allow you to fall under Maaliks's[14] guardianship,

For how can Heaven be Heaven without you in it?

---

[13] The angel of death

[14] The angel who guardians Hell

Hate For Love / Love For Hate

You claim to hate that which I love,
Yet that which I love loves you more than you could
comprehend,
He knows that it is in fact you that you hate,
And His mercy is open for you until the very end.

You claim to hate that which I love,
And then you call that which I love the one who hates,
Maybe you are confused as to what He is,
For such love I don't think you can contemplate.

You claim to hate those that He loves,
When those He loves want to bring His love to you,
They pray there is no seal on your heart,
I so wish you could see His way as I do.

So, do you hate me for loving love?
Do you hate me for wanting to go to our source?
How can I then fight for love with hate,
When you fight love without no remorse?

Do you judge me for following a book,
Of which you have not even read a word?
Are you jealous like the cow,
Trapped behind a fence looking up at the bird?

Why do you fear us so much?
When all we want to show you is the love,
That we have for each other,
And for the One high up above?

I forgive you cos we know,
If we forgive others, He'll forgive you,
But if you try to hurt us then I'll fight,
Even though we hate it, it's something we must do.

A Wife That

I want a wife who listens to me,
A wife who has the same vision as me,
A wife who is as giving as me,
A wife who is on the same mission as me,

I want a wife who doesn't get jealous,
Or do the same with me with other fellers,
I want a girl who's a rebel like I am,
And with whom I can have a proper conversation,

I want a wife who is on her deen,
Who won't teach my kids that God is three,
Or say God died on a cross for me,
That will take my daughters to the mosque for me,

I want a wife who doesn't act deceiving,
Who shows love and doesn't just receive it,
Who when I tell her I care she actually believes it,
A wife that shares my dream and will strive to achieve it,

I want a wife who isn't gassed by the TV,
Who when times are hard makes them easy,
That at least likes some of my CD's,
That hasn't always got to get her way so greedy,

A wife that isn't too closed in,
A wife that isn't scared to show her emotions,
Not just when *she's* upset and feels broken,
A wife whose heart doesn't seem so frozen,

Not a wife filled with paranoia,
That at the wedding vows will probably bring her lawyer,
A girl with whom my success won't annoy her,
That doesn't put me down when I don't have an
employer,

I want a wife who fits just like a glove,
And you fit none of the criteria above,
I guess all I can do is shrug,
And wonder why it's with you my heart has fallen in
love?

How & When

How can we live with ourselves when our brothers are dying?
How can we smile when our mothers are crying?
How can we rest when our Ummah is trying,
So hard to break free from oppression in Palestine?

How can we allow this to continue to happen?
How can all you care about be the Duniya's distractions?
How can we stay silent in our words and our actions?
How can we fight each other over political factions?

How can we feel good when our Ummahs in pain?
How can we fight each other when our enemy is one and the same?
How can the blood not boil inside our veins,
When the blood of our sisters pours like rain?

When we are inactive how can we moan?
How can we sleep with so much chaos back home?
How can we rest when there's a child alone,
Because her parents were killed by one of Obama's drones?

Seriously how can the tears not pour like rivers,
When you see what they have done to us in Libya?

How long will we just wait for Allah to deliver us,
Before we fight the jihad from the Islam He has given
us?

How can our leaders be so useless?
How long can we just accept their excuses?
How many more human rights abuses?
Arghhh the pain when they use our own brothers to
shoot us!

How did the nation of Islam end up in this state,
From a nation of which none has ever been as great?
How can we celebrate iftar with so much food on our
plates,
When there are those of us without clean water or
dates?

When will they stop their continues attack?
When will they finally leave alone Iraq?
When will they stop causing mischief on every land on
the map?
When will we chase them away so that they never come
back?

When will we cut out the cancer where the Middle East
is?
Which will keep growing til the land it consumes
reaches,

From the Euphrates in Iraq to the Nile in Egypt,
How can now with 1.6 billion Muslims we be at our
weakest?

How can we live of the fruits of imperialism,
On the lands where our people are living?
How can we sit back whilst they rape our religion?
Soon you'll have to make a decision, how can you not
choose Allahs cause as your mission?

Our Nation

Where the sun sets,
To where it does rise,
A nation rose,
So large in size,

With mighty Caliphs,
And scholars wise,
One nation,
Under one God in the skies.

Justice spread,
With human rights,
A beacon of justice,
Did ignite,
A world marvelled,
At our nations might,
Rose from the bottom,
To such amazing heights.

From the lions,
To the ants,
From the jungles,
To the desert sands,
From the Chinese border,
To the South of France,
We stood united,
Within the motherland.

The land was split,
Like an earthquake,

A once mighty nation,
Now many states,
Everything we owned,
They did take,
But the bond of the shuhada,
They can never break.

It Hurts To Know

It's strange how memories still haunt me,

And how everywhere I go memories of you taunt me,

Cos it seems like I have a memory of us being there together,

And these memories will linger there forever,

I remember so many things some good and some bad,

Like your face when you're mad or your voice when you're sad,

Your smile when you thought I would say something cheesy,

Or your smile when you were feeling like being cheeky,

You had such a beautiful smile but underneath there,

Was a pain in your eyes that you'd never share,

To be honest today I doubt that you even care,

But let me still remind you of some things I remember,

I remember you'd call me four five times a day,

I remember our conversations and things you'd say,

I remember your voice when you'd sing and hit the deep notes,

I remember early morning waiting with you in Heathrow,

I remember a time when I kept my phone,

On loudspeaker all night cos you said you didn't want to be alone,

I remember how we used to playfight in your yard......,

Oh wait I remember you "don't live in a yard" you "live in a home",

I remember when you'd lie with legs on my lap whilst we watched telly,

Or when we'd lie on your bed with my head on your belly,

I remember when we used to hug,

The really long ones, the ones I used to love,

I remember when you'd hit me in the most painful spot,

But the painful memories and heartache I also never forgot,

How I'd beg when I'd pray that these feelings would stop,

Now that think about it you really used to put me down a lot,

But you want to know what really stings?

That when its comes to you I remember so many things,

Like the day I fell in love or when we first met,

But you'll probably never remember these things I'll never forget.

Children of Adam

Were there noone left in the world with a conscience,
And the idea of human rights was seen as old fashioned
nonsense,
Were the media to call my peaceful means acts of terror,
And I was alone in this world on my endeaver,
Were people to spit at me in the streets,
And never listen to a word I say whenever I'd speak,
Were they to try make me turn my back I could never
let them,
For they are the children of Adam how can I forget
them,

Even if they were to hang me in Trafalgar Square,
And I struggled to stay conscious out of fear,
Even when trying to find hope seems hopeless,
And I they drugged me up so much I couldn't even
focus,
Even if they gave me a choice between London
Dungeon,
Or the stolen wealth of the tower of London,
Were they to try give me amnesia I could never let them,
For they are the children of Adam how can I forget
them,

If I ever lived when kindness was seen as a weakness,
And I was the only one left who believed this,
If my cause was seen as a type of mental illness,
And I became a pariah in my community because I feel
this,
If my body was so exhausted I could barely move,
And the only options put in front of me was quit or

loose,
Then they offered to put the sun in right hand and the
moon in my left,
Still they are the children of Adam how can I forget the
oppressed,

Shaytan In The Middle

She may have seemed cute,
That's why I never suspected.
She may have seemed nice,
That's why she weren't detected.

But looks are deceiving,
I said it but didn't see,
I was blinded by her charm,
But that's all it was for me.

Sometimes I think it may,
Have been partly my fault,
Maybe I led her on in a way,
Or maybe her heart was broke.

But I swear I made it clear,
But maybe words just aren't enough,
And my actions didn't match them,
Maybe she was in love or lust.

Yet maybe she's just jealous,
Or maybe she is straight evil,
Instigating dividing friends,
Playing around with people.

And I tried to be a good friend,
And good friends you don't avoid them.
She may have poisoned your mind against me,
But your mind was weak enough to be poisoned.

Her scheming and her plotting,
Was revealed but it weren't just me,
She did it too the others,
But you chose to not trust me.

Shaytan can seem so sweet,
But if he didn't how could he deceive,
If he showed you who he was,
You would just tell him "Leave!"

I guess you girls stick together,
So you'll believe her evil plots,
But maybe in the distant future,
You'll look back and join the dots,

And then you'll understand,
Why she turned you against me,
Then you'll realise the truth,
That I was not the real enemy.

Searching

On a cold March morning she sat in the park,
Picked a flower and started plucking petals,
He loves me, he loves me not, he loves me,
He loves me not is how it ended but her heart was a rebel.
She felt the flower smelt as sweet as his words,
But the plants that would represent him would more likely be nettles,
For he would sting her heart, like many before him,
Change up his behavior like Dr Hyde and Mr. Jekyll.
Been searching for so long, but she'd never give up,
Been searching for so long and never lost hope,
For what could be better in this life then being in love,
Long hugs, strolling by the river and reading love notes?
He seemed to be a hero like Achilles,
But was more likely her Achilles heel.
He promised her love and stole her heart,
What more precious an item could he steal?
It felt like she was going out of her mind,
She was searching for love, but love is blind,
It's something if you search for you will never find,
You have to just wait, cos love comes with time.

Late at night she lay awake in her bed,
Her head started to drift to sweet memories,
Feeling alone she knew she must sleep,
Instead of staying up listening to sad love melodies.
She remembered when she first met her ex,
He seemed to speak away her pain like her remedy,
But he ended up being more pain in the end,
Still she kept searching, where does she find the energy.

She got up and looked out the window,
At the street below, but looking more at her reflection,
Would the person opposite always stay single?
Were happy endings in love just a Hollywood invention?
Her heart was broken into a thousand pieces,
It almost stopped beating needing a resurrection,
She had suffered a lovesickness so bad,
A sickness that couldn't be fixed with an injection.
It felt like she was going out of her brain,
She was searching for love, but love is pain,
Her tears had fallen before like rain,
But no amount of tears could put out the flame.

A lone tear rolled out her eye,
She was alone here trying not to cry,
Put the phone to her ear, once again to try,
On unknown number hoping he'd pick up this time,
His answer phone message reminded her of his voice,
And it sent a shiver running down her spine,
And now even though she knew she wasn't his choice,
She felt like leaving a message shouting down the line.
You see the pain was a deep burning in her heart,
A none stop burning, burning like the fires of hell,
Nothing could put out the fire that was burning,
Not even all the rivers, lakes and oceans in the world.
The fire made it easy for her heart to melt,
She told herself that love was a type of mental health,
But was it love or lack of love that she wanted to feel?
Did she want to fall in love or just to love herself?
It felt like she was going out of her head,
She was searching for love, but she was misled,
She was searching for love to heal her heart that bled,
But it was love for herself that she needed instead.

Somewhere I Belong

I was born and raised here, as British as can be,
But the British Nationalist Party would disagree,
And I find it hard to pledge allegiance to the Queen,
When the oppression she represents goes against my
deen,
And if I oppose British foreign policy I'm called a
traitor,
But when my dad left Sudan it was under British
occupation,
Whose divide and conquer tactics are still present and
from it Sudan still suffers,
So if I'm not a traitor to one am I a traitor to the other?

Or what about when a British funded Junta kicked my
dad out of Greece,
Do I thank Britain for the accepting the asylum he
seeked,
Still I'm a born and bred Londoner and proud of that
fact,
When they tell me to "Go back home", I say I'm already
back,
And I feel pride whenever I hear British rap,
I like to have a cup of English tea with my kebab wrap,
I used to look for somewhere I belong like Linkin Park,
Before I realized I need look no further than Finsbury
Park.

Bun Da Gun, Vibes Not Knives

Bun Da Gun, Vibes Not Knives,
She wept under the pale moonlight,
She lost her son her only child,
And she continued to weep all through the night.
All of a sudden she felt alone,
How could her son be killed out here on road?
And it seemed like her husband didn't care,
But he was just trying to stay strong for her.
After she raised him all on her own,
Taught him all that she did know,
And another yout pulled a leng and pulled the trigger,
Now she's lost the only thing she lived for.
Into the hands of God, he was delivered,
That dark dark night she cried a river,
Then she looked to the sky and felt a shiver,
That's when she knew that God was with her.

So, Bun Da Gun, Vibes Not Knives,
This a dedication to those who lost their lives,
And their mums and wives,
Just think of all they could have done if they were still
alive.

Bun Da Gun, Vibes Not Knives,
Our young are split into different tribes,
The system wants to see us divide,
In the jungle of the concrete high rise.
It started with a bad look,
Now neither wants to act like they're shook,
But it ended with another kid getting jukked,

It ended with another life being took.
Damilola was killed only ten years old,
Anaka Pinto on Tottenham High Road,
Nas, for being in the wrong postcode,
It took five youts to murder Kojo.
And I don't know the reason for this grieving,
Why's a yout on the floor bleeding,
Leaking as the lord takes his soul,
Another yout swallowed up by the road.

So, Bun Da Gun, Vibes Not Knives,
This a dedication to those who lost their lives,
And their mums and wives,
Just think of all they could have done if they were still alive.

Bun Da Gun, Vibes Not Knives,
There's a problem from which we can't run and ride,
Whole families are ruined when guns collide,
Another news broadcast as another son dies.
And I don't know why another mum must cry,
Another dad must feel sad at the loss of a child.
From all this mad chaos we must rise,
Just know God's looking down on us from the sky,
And God feels our pain,
He cries so many teardrops we call them rain,
And every drop in every bloodstain,
And the culprits ain't the only ones to blame.
We live under a system that needs to change,
What could drive a yout to act so insane,
And take another yout's life when it comes to beef,
We need to bring peace to London's streets.

America's Letter

Hi I'm America, this is my letter to mankind,
Your enemy but we were friends at one time,
We were one you and I with the trees and animals,
You didn't need material things for our bond was more
valuable,
I supplied you with everything you needed to survive,
You showed me respect, we were in love for a time,
I loved to hear your innocent laugh, I loved to see you
smile,
You, me, the trees and animals were all entwined,
That was our time,

But then your evil side came across the seas,
In boats made of dead trees like a swarm of bees,
Your symbol now the cross with which you killed your
own god,
And you killed yourselves by the thousand in an orgy of
blood.

Covered me with concrete til I couldn't even breath,
If you listened with your hearts not your ears you would
have heard me scream,
Enslaved yourselves, I became a haven for your
plantations,
Went from being the most good to the most evil of
nations.

Sold me off in pieces like I was ever yours to own,

Carved your faces in the rocks and mountains, my bones,
As you drilled holes inside of me to suck out my blood,
And use it for planes and tanks, your mechanical thugs,
And used them for wars to create your empires birth,
Made me the most hated of lands on the entire earth,
Built cities to pollute my air and rivers,
I loved you so much but now I don't think I can ever forgive ya.

So if I quake it's you who's caused my heart to break,
I can't defend myself any other way this is all I can take,
My flag and national anthem are yours not mine,
They represent what did and what you did to me was a crime.

And you blame me every time another bomb hits,
Mankind your internal conflicts are causing your conscripts,
To use me as an excuse to fight in my brothers Africa and Asia,
And strip them of their resources for my trees paper.

I was once in love with my people,
But now this new you I just see as evil,
And you keep saying you love me but how can I believe you,
Put your hand on your hearts and sing for me, but you just sound deceitful.

Celebrate your victory over me on thanksgiving,

You use me like a pimp uses women,
Rape me none stop like you always on Viagra,
Whilst my tears never stop falling in Niagara,

Hi I'm America, this is my letter to mankind,
Your enemy but we were friends at one time,
We were one you and I with the trees and animals,
You didn't need material things for our bond was more valuable,
I supplied you with everything you needed to survive,
You showed me respect, we were in love for a time,
I loved to hear your innocent laugh, I loved to see you smile,
You, me, the trees and animals were all entwined,
That was our time,

Best Left Unsaid

It hit me like a bullet,
I really weren't prepared,
Cos I didn't realise til then,
Exactly how much I cared.
I wanted to tell you stop,
And be with me instead,
But some things are worth saying,
And some best left unsaid.

I felt it in my stomach,
I felt it in my brain,
My soul was left shaking,
And my heart was left in pain.
I really want to tell you,
What's going on in my head,
But some things are worth saying,
And some best left unsaid.

And so you'll never know,
What I've kept quiet for these years,
Cos what the point in saying,
When it'll just make things weird.
Even if it never stops,
I'll keep it quiet til I'm dead,
Cos some things are worth saying,
And some best left unsaid.

I wonder if at one time,
I may have had a shot,
I guess there's no point in thinking

Like that, if I did it's been forgot.
What's the point in writing,
You a poem you'll have never read?
Cos some things are worth saying,
And some best left unsaid.

So I'll smile when I see you,
And act like life's a joke,
Cos what's the point in trying,
When I haven't got a hope.
I'll have to keep laughing,
Whilst my heart is torn to shreds,
Cos some things are worth saying,
And some best left unsaid.

I hope that he sees,
You the same way that I do,
Cos you're not the type to settle for,
He'd be so lucky to have you.
It's best to wish for that,
Then be hanging by a thread,
Cos some things are worth saying,
And some best left unsaid.

Maybe you'll invite me to your wedding,
Maybe I'll attend,
Cos whatever happens,
I'd rather have you as a friend.
Maybe I'll be happy,
For you as you're wed,
Some things are worth saying,
But some best left unsaid.

Is It Wrong?

Is it wrong to turn down those who want me,
To wait for one who doesn't seem to care?
Is it selfish to only want the best?
I mean, why should I be the one to have her?

Is it wrong to wait patiently for something,
That is an almost impossible possibility?
Or is it wrong to give up on that person,
And settle for someone with more availability?

Is it wrong to make dua[15] to have her,
Knowing in order to do so she must split with her man?
Cos in essence that's what you're asking Allah,
Will that cause me to be crowned by the Shaytan?

Is it wrong to try and win her heart,
If you know her father wouldn't accept you,
And it could cause strife amongst a family?
Is it not just to him but to her disrespectful?

Is it wrong to want her,
When I have nothing to offer that he can't?
I have no great wealth, fame or future,
All I can offer is my heart.

Is it wrong to love her?
Is it wrong to blame her for this depression?
Do I even have the right to love her?
Oh Allah please answer these questions.

---

[15] Asking God for something

Because I love her so much,
That I feel completely lost,
How can this feeling be wrong,
When it feels like it's worth any cost?

So please have some mercy on my heart,
Oh Rahman[16] tell me what I must do,
Otherwise I don't know how I can survive,
Do I even have the right to ask any of this from You?

---

[16] One of the 99 names of God, meaning The Most Merciful

Sam Sterling

Born in Jamaica he came to London by boat,
A generation who came to a city of hope,
But discrimination infected it like a virus,
On the shops they wrote no dogs, no blacks, no Irish.

He got a job in his first week and then became a chef,
He lived in one room, but for his family a four bedroom
house he left,
He came from a generation where you showed each
other respect,
But to today's generation respect means your cred.

He had a happy life, so we should celebrate that,
He was a man of God, so to God he will go back,
He lost his parents when he was young,
But was still a family man for his wife, daughters and
son.

When Clim fell ill he looked after her still,
And raised his grandkids as well when Sheila was killed,
So his house was always a busy home,
And he was at peace before he died for he never died
alone.

RIP Samuel Sterling, may God have mercy on your soul
(1927-2012)

Part 2

A Bench

Foreword

In the name of Allah, Most Gracious, Most Merciful, Lord of all that exists.
Through Him we seek guidance and ask that he grants us love in our hearts and protects us from hatred, both hatred against us and hatred by us.

His prophet Muhammad (may Allah's peace and blessings be upon him) came across an old lady, who repeatedly slandered him, not knowing that it was in fact him that she was speaking too. She was leaving Mecca because of the division within it, of which she blamed him. But instead of responding with hate, he responded by helping her to move, carrying her stuff for her, pitching her tent, finding her food and cooking for her, all the while she continued to insult him, whilst not knowing who he truly was. Only when he left her did she ask who he was and when he told her she said: "I bear witness that there is no god but Allah and that Muhammad is his messenger". He had defeated hate with love.

I wanted to write a story of the battle between love and hate, and as a poet I decided to write it as a poem. Although the characters are not Muslim, in fact they are very loosely based on the great poets; Pablo Neruda and Maya Angelou, and although I didn't want to write an Islamic poem, but rather a poem that anyone can relate to, I used verses of the Qur'an and hadeeth (sayings of the prophet Muhammad to back up my points. This is because I am a Muslim and my point of view will therefore be a Muslim point of view, even if it is my personal understanding of Islam.

I find it sad that today I see so much hatred in people, including by many Muslims and Christians, and wanted to offer a critique of hatred and show that whilst *anger* can be a force for good sometimes, *hatred* on the other hand is a self-defeating emotion.

As well as sources from Islam there is a line based on the quote of Confucius which says: "Before you embark on a journey of revenge, dig two graves." Although more a philosophy, many people consider Confucianism to be a form of religion.

I was heavily inspired by the thirteenth century Persian poet Nizami Ganjavi, whom is one of my favourite poets and whose version of "Layla and Majnun/Qays" is one of the greatest love poems ever written.

Although much of the poem is set in a western nation and some other within a South American country, I tried not to imply there were any particular countries. This gave me more freedom, although I was inspired by the Cuban Revolution, the Bolivarian Revolution in Venezuela and the current situation in Colombia with FARC rebels fighting against a western backed dictatorship.

As well as loosely basing the two main characters on poets, I named another Jalal in tribute to Jalaluddin Rumi, although the character of Jalal bears no relation to that of Rumi.

Although I have been writing poetry for many years, this is my first attempt at such a long poem, so I hope that you enjoy it and that you get something out of it.

A Bench

A bench
A bench in a park
In a park dangerous after dark
Yet this bench was the start
Of a tale of the heart

The sky was blue with the sun drooping low and,
The wind was ever so gently blowing,
The air smelled like the perfume of a rose,
Soon the day would be coming to a close,

A girl,
A girl alone with her tears,
Alone with her tears escaping her eyes,
Out of sorrow for her mother had died,
So, she sat on the bench and cried,

The pain it consumed her soul,
Where there was once happiness there was a hole,
And it seemed like this pain would last forever,
For how could such a wound ever get better?

A boy,
A boy out of breath,
Out of breath from his sports,
So, he left from the court,
Sat on the bench and captured his thoughts,

Nine years old yet thought he was a man,
Holding the basketball in his hand,

He heard the girl about his age beside him,
And he noticed that she was crying,

A choice,
A choice whether to ignore her,
Whether to ignore her tears or ask what's wrong,
A decision for which he couldn't take long,
And his decision would change the path both their lives
were on,

For Allah is the Best Of Planners and fate,
Means the effects of our choice only He contemplates,
At the time a choice may seem small,
But a butterfly flapping its wings can cause empires to
fall,

"Sorry"
"Sorry for what?"
"For whatever has caused you to weep"
And whilst the tears rolled down her cheek,
He leaned forward and offered her a sweet,

She looked at him and for a moment it did seem,
Like all her problems in life had been a bad dream,
And although the moment had gone in a flash,
Something had grown in her heart that would continue
to last,

A word,
Not a word was said,
Was said after those words,
Yet even though not even one was heard,
More was said than in the longest verse,

Even though he knew not what made her cry,
He felt pain like never before without knowing why,
All he knew was that it had caused her distress,
And this girl whoever she was deserved to be blessed,

She smiled,
She smiled though overcome with sadness,
Such sadness, for a moment though she forgot her grief,
As she wiped her eyes upon her sleeve,
Then when he left she continued to watch him leave,

Despite losing her mother she could be forgiven,
That now she felt a ray of hope that life was worth living,
And she asked God to let her see him again,
For she knew that right now she needed a friend,

A name,
He asked her name the next time they met,
"My name is Maya" is what she replied,
He smiled and said that "Pablo is mine"
And this is how the friendship started at age nine,

It had been two weeks since they had first spoke,
And Pablo had gone to the bench every day in hope,
That he would get to see if she was okay,
And so they spoke for hours upon that day,

Again,
Again the two of them met,
And then again they met on the bench every weekend,
Over time their conversations became more intense,
And soon they became the best of friends,

It was like they were a two-person team,
Wherever people saw Pablo Maya was seen,
They backed each other when one would fight,
And would speak on the bench deep into the night,

A kiss,
A kiss on that same bench,
On that bench after four years of friendship,
Pablo told her he loved her and really meant it,
It felt like their love was never ending,

For love is a word often misunderstood,
Often those think they have fallen but really its lust,
But for Pablo and Maya love was spiritual,
If they didn't speak for a day the day was miserable,

No one
"No one else can compare" said Pablo
"Can compare to you, my one and only
No one else knows me the way you know me
Please don't you ever leave me lonely"

"That is one thing I will never do"
Said Maya "And I swear I'll never lie to you
For I trust you more than I trusted anyone ever
Promise me that we'll always be together"

"Always,
Always for now and forever
For now and forever until I take my last breath
I will stand by you even in death
If you lost everything you'd still have me left

You have taken a permanent residence in my heart
And nothing or no one can keep us apart
Not even an army fifty-thousand strong
Can keep me from being with you it's where I belong"

In love,
Deeper in love they fell,
They fell into a bottomless ocean,
And they were drowning together in the emotion,
They became lost in each other's devotion

Nothing else mattered to Pablo only Maya,
Like a moth he was drawn only to her fire,
But unlike that unlucky creature the flame was drawn to him too,
To Maya Pablo was all that she knew,

In time,
In time the relationship would grow,
Ten years passed and they got more close,
Then on her 19th birthday he gave her a rose,
Got on one knee and then he proposed,

"For the only love that I've ever known,
If I don't marry you I'd rather be alone,
Complete me like the moon completes the night,
And do me the honour of becoming my wife"

Perfect,
Everything was going perfect,
Maya was so happy that her face glowed,
Her father took one look at her and did know,

He could read her like a poem they were that close,

How more smoothly could a love story go?
For what was about to happen how could they know?
So happy and ecstatic nothing else mattered,
They thought they would live happily ever after,
BUT

A truth,
A truth hidden so deep,
But one darker than a starless night,
Maya's father had stolen Pablo's father's life,
When Pablo was six months old in a meaningless fight,

What a senseless death, what a twist of fate,
That a crime so old would cause two hearts to break,
Twenty years later how could their children be in love,
Who could have known but our lord up above?

Maybe
Maybe it was destiny
Destiny that they would meet and become engaged
At the stag Pablo's cousin recognised Maya's fathers face
And after that he became enraged

How could that man be laughing and joking
After leaving his uncle on the floor dying and choking?
How could he allow this wedding too take place?
So he told Pablo the horrible truth to his face,

He ran
Pablo ran when he heard the news
Ran none stop through street after street

He didn't know how to stop the pain was too deep
Never was there a situation so bleak

How could such a horror be true?
How could the girl that he loved more than he knew
Be the daughter of one who had caused a tragedy?
How could such a perfect love descend into such
anarchy?

Revenge!
When plotting revenge dig two graves,
Pablo's anger just could not be quenched
Inside it burnt like a stick of incense
The start of such a tragic set of events

It burnt throughout his arteries
Nothing could now leave his heart in peace,
It got so strong that even he was amazed
For he never knew that there could exist such a rage,

Now what?
Now what could Pablo do?
Pablo thought it through fiddling with his ring,
Things had been so perfect but now with the sin
Her father had committed there was no forgiving,

See it was love versus hate which one would he choose,
Anger can be like oil depending on how it's used,
If controlled it can make an engine run,
But a single spark and it's more dangerous than a gun,

MURDER!
Murder was on Pablo's mind

He confronted his nemesis in an alleyway,
Maya's father begged forgiveness her his daughter's sake
But the anger was far more than Pablo could take,

He looked into the eyes of the father of she he loved,
And knew that he could not forgive this grudge,
He thought of Maya and hesitated for a second,
But then put his hand in his jacket and felt his weapon,

A life
A life is such a beautiful gift
Yet oh how easily it can be lost
So he pulled out the knife in the blistering frost
And took a life regardless of the cost,

He paused for a second, what had he done?
Everything he had achieved with Maya was now gone,
She would never understand why he done it,
He fell into unhappiness's deep deep summit,

A text
A text was sent to Maya's phone
"I'm sorry" it read she didn't know for what,
She tried to phone him, but his phone was off,
So, Maya panicked feeling at a loss

Even though it was only an apology she knew,
That it must be something serious that he did do,
What could it be? Thoughts plagued her mind,
But nothing prepared her for what she would find,

The news
The news tore Maya's heart into pieces

It turned her soul colder than ice
So many times she contemplated suicide
But such a beautiful gift must go on: life

How could the one who comforted her when,
All those years ago she had lost one of her parents,
Be the same man who will take the other?
How could he hate him who she loved, but love her?

Anger
Anger engulfed her completely
How in all the heavens could he do this to her?
They were meant to be in love, but did he really care?
O why was life so harsh and unfair?

O how the duniya[17] can be so cruel
The way Shaytan[18] can use hate as a tool
To turn a man in love into a hateful fool
Who'll break Allah's 5th commanding rule

Years passed
Years passed Pablo had gone on the run
Maya married her uncle's friend a man called Chad
But the bitterness and hatred drove her mad
For the man she once loved but had killed her dad,

She barely spoke always looking like a sad case,
And the depression she felt was always on her face,
In those years she would just randomly cry

---

[17] Duniya is Arabic for "World", however in Islam it can be broadened to mean
our current existence and the false desires and temptations that exist within it.

[18] An Arabic name for the devil

And when her mouth smiled there was sadness in her
eyes

Despair
Maya could not move for despair
In the end Chad decided to get her
Involved in helping make her community better
And fight for their rights united together

For her people were victims of police brutality
And society infected with a white supremacist insanity
Discrimination had seeped into every aspect of life
After five-hundred years of slavery and genocide

Pregnant
She fell pregnant
Pregnant with Chad's baby only about six months
After Pablo had fled and gone on the run
Soon she was going to have a daughter or son

And now without either Pablo or her father
She would soon have a son or a daughter
And once again someone to live for
At least one dream came true from all that she'd wished
for

She read
She read books about her people's plight
She read about her people's glorious history
And African nations that existed before slavery
And suddenly she began to unravel the mysteries

She decided to fight to regain the honour lost

And help her people regardless of the cost
She became a respected historian and author
But still she missed Pablo as the desert misses water

Yet hate
Yet hate still consumed her
He had betrayed their love as evil as a demon
He had chosen hate over their love now she had to get even
Nothing could quench the hate she was feeling

Still for hours out the window she would look
Still she kept the rose he'd given her pressed in a book
Still she could not look at it, not even once
Scared she might still feel something she pretended was gone

Teaching
She began teaching at university
Teaching history and English literature
She became the universities first black female lecturer
And more and more grew peoples respect for her

Through all this the television interviewed her
And she was seen on the interview by one who knew her
Who knew her many many years before
But now he no longer knew her no more

A War
A war halfway across the globe
A war for justice and liberation
A war in the land of his parents' creation
A war Pablo fought in his mother nation

Where injustice and oppression was the law
And the only democracy was revolutionary war
Where it was a crime to speak of rights
Where starving mothers knew only sleepless nights

Bullets
Bullets flew by as he fought
Many of his friends had been killed
But in Pablo no fear had been instilled
For he was dead inside now unable to feel

What else was left for him to live for?
When you have nothing how easy it is to risk all
Here Pablo had found a cause he did believe in
Here the only care of the heart was that it kept beating

A dream
A dream plagued his mind
The same dream he dreamt every night
An impossible dream for which he'd be willing to fight
But there are some wrongs you just can't put right

Was it a dream or was it a nightmare?
When he awoke he felt that she was right there
But o how unfortunate he felt each morning
Once the truth of the situation began dawning

One time
One time a group of soldiers
A group of soldiers came close Pablo's position
And with his band he managed to hit them
Whilst they dropped Pablo didn't regret his decision

Yet one pulled himself up and did cry:
"I have a daughter waiting for me I must not die"
So Pablo shot him again but again he stood
"I have a daughter at home" he repeated not giving up

Shooting
Pablo continued shooting the man
But still he dragged his mangled body across the dirt
"I have a daughter I must get back to her
I'm all she has left, my death I must avert"

Pablo was moved but he had to finish the mission
Otherwise the soldier could give away their position
So he put his gun right up against the man's heart
And then with his eyes shut he let the gun spark

The wake
At the man's wake Pablo watched on
Pablo watched on from a great distance
He saw a small girl crying as she missed him
And people tried to pull her away as she kissed him

Pablo also wept as he beheld the harrowing sight
And he wondered: 'Is what I am doing really right?'
He was creating a better world but at what cost?
Why should these soldiers die just to protect their boss?

Once More
Once More he regretted
Regretted killing a man for his daughter's sake
The irony was too much for Pablo to take
Was this how Maya had been at her father's wake?

Did she cry as this little girl did cry?
Did she repeatedly keep asking why?
Did she look like the sun would never again shine?
Just as she'd looked when they'd first met aged nine

The child
The child stayed after
Stayed after the wake all by herself
For without her father she had no one else
But from a distance Pablo did stay as well

For a few weeks he refused to fight
As he could no longer justify to himself taking a life
But as the death toll reached a quarter of a million
He decided that taking one more life could end the killing

Showdown
A showdown took place
Took place between him and the head of state
After Pablo had climbed over his gate
Both tried to fire, but from death only one would escape

The foreign backed dictator fell to floor
In this single act they saw an end to the war
He'd seen so many bodies that the death didn't affect him
The de-sensitization of death did now infect him

Freedom
Freedom's something all men have a right too
But in many places they don't have that right

Yet where there's oppression a revolutionary fire ignites
And Pablo's people had eventually won their fight

For it is better to die on your feet than live on your
knees[19]
What could be the worth of anything if you're not free?
It's better living a life of freedom with troubles
Than to live in subjugation without any struggles[20]

Success
Success is so sweet and celebrations
Poured into the streets with joy and hope
People laughing, dancing and telling jokes
But one stayed quiet his heart still broke

Broken into a thousand shards
Scattered across the world like the night sky with stars
He couldn't admit how much he regretted his decision
To pick hate over love, to his heart he should have
listened

Her laugh
Her laugh still rung in his ears
Her face was still etched on his mind
Her smile still appeared when he closed his eyes
He couldn't forget them no matter how he tried

They followed him wherever he went teasing his mind

---

[19] This line is a quote by South American revolutionary Ernesto "Che" Guevara

[20] These two lines are based on a quote by former the former president of Guinea: Sekou Toure

Reminding him of what he lost and they say love can be
blind
But hate is always blinding to the point where logic and
reason
Are forgot and towards your own self you commit
treason

Music
Music was playing in the park
Maya sat on the bench from this story's beginning
Her mind strayed for a split second to when she kissed
him
But she wouldn't allow herself to admit that she missed
him

O for how could one miss her greatest nemesis?
What she felt before he murdered her father had no
relevance
Her hero had now become a monster
Her sunshine had turned into her rain and thunder

His voice
His voice she still heard in the wind
His eyes were imprinted upon her memory
And how could she ever forget his energy?
But also how could she ever forget he was now her
enemy?

She tried to make herself plot revenge in her head
She tried to make herself wish that he was dead
Yet however much she tried part of her still loved him
When she felt at her lowest she remembered how she
used to hug him

A Child
A child, the son of Maya and Chad
Jalal was his name and now he was ten,
Yet at this early age he started plotting revenge
On he who killed his grandfather, though he weren't
born then

Yet he saw his mother crying over him
Jalal vowed that he would never forget the sin
That had destroyed his mother and turned her into a
shell
Who had took her from happiness and into hell

One Day
One day Jalal and Maya in her study
Were playing when Jalal knocked over a book
And what fell out, o how Maya's heart shook
It was the rose when he did propose on the bench by the
brook

Suddenly all the memories began flowing
And the water in her eyes began growing
She wept so hard even Jalal started as well
Not knowing the reason why his mother was crying like a
little girl

Six years
Six years later and Jalal almost forgot
But many times he was reminded as he grew
As he heard his mother cry alone in her room
But of Pablo's past love he hadn't a clue

For it was a secret of which no one did speak
It's like those years together had got delete
So anger overcame him and the chain did endure
For hate breeds hate and it can destroy even the pure

A Trip
A family trip to a foreign land
Maya, Chad and Jalal gone to see the revolution
But the former coloniser had threatened to nuke them
And that happened to be the same country that they had
grew in

So emotions were high and Chad and Maya were feeling
Nervous about how the people would receive them
Despite Maya and Chad opposing their own government
Some people still blamed the imperialist country's
residents

The Land
The land made Maya think of Pablo
Knowing this was the land from whom he descended
She saw a nation proud of their new independence
Although with the imperialists there were growing
tensions

For the imperialists will never accept full liberation
And allow their former colony self determination
For sometimes freedom must come from fighting evil
This is not hate for your enemy but love for your people

Kidnapped
Kidnapped from their hotel room
A family terrified and held prisoner

The leader of the plot got a shock when he came to visit them
What were the chances: one in a million?

How out of all the tourists that came to their state
Could it be her that they caught, was it fate?
For the Best Of Planners[21] does not do nothing by chance
But who but Him could ever understand these plans?

Collapsed
Maya collapsed on the floor in shock
O how the tears overwhelmed her at the sight
Whilst Pablo, the plots leader turned pale and white
Wanting to say something but his lips remained quiet

He stood and stared like 'was this a dream?'
Had she planned it, was this one of her schemes?
He saw her husband and son and felt a jealousy
Stronger than ever before draining his energy

The shock
The shock was still felt by Maya
Oh what a cruel twist of fate had occurred
To Chad and Jalal she didn't say a word
About who Pablo was and who he was to her

Overcome with emotions in a confusing state
A mixture of joy and sadness, love and hate
Were they enemies or were they not?
She still loved him, but what he did she never forgot

---

[21] Allah is described as "The Best Of Planners" in the Qur'an (3:54, 8:30)

Oh Why?
"Oh why did you ruin everything?"
Days later she had to ask
"He killed my father, how could I let that pass?"
Replied Pablo and then he left the cell so fast

How could she not understand his reasons?
To do nothing to avenge his father would have been treason
For family comes first even if he never knew him
Even if it meant that his own plans were ruined

It's Him
'It's him' realised Jalal
So many times he pictured this before
And it was revenge that Jalal had swore
Next time that Pablo walked through the door

He would keep it secret from Maya and Chad
Knowing that if they knew that they would get mad
For such an act was practically suicide
But all Jalal could think of was how his mother had cried

Ambush
Jalal tried to ambush Pablo
Attacked him with a knife when he entered the cell
Ran at him screaming "See you in hell"
But Pablo punched him and unconscious he fell

The room fell silent for a couple of anxious seconds
Pablo then picked up Jalal's fallen weapon

Pondering how Jalal had been smart enough to conceal it
And how close he came to death he could almost feel it

Justice
Justice must be done for the attack
"Don't he's your son!" Maya then cried
But with only one look into her eyes
He knew her well enough to know it was a lie

For a second, even after all that had occurred
Pablo was disappointed that she didn't stick to her word
When they had promised to never lie to each other
But he couldn't blame her for being a protective mother

Now what?
Now what could he do?
Jalal had attacked him with a razor
Now Pablo had to kill this teenager
But he had Maya's eyes not the eyes of a stranger

He remembered the tears in those eyes when they first met
And the stars he saw in them he'd never forget
Like two moons reflecting the suns light
And how could the killing of a child be right?

He left
So, he left Jalal alone
For so long he pretended he no longer cared
But when he had seen Maya sitting there
It was a situation for which he wasn't prepared

"I miss you" he told her when he could no longer take it
"How dare you say that after my heart you did break it?"
And Maya slapped him so hard half his face went red
"How dare you, because of you my father is dead!"

"Sorry"
To say sorry, he found so hard
"I let my hate overpower my love
I threw away our future because of my grudge
When I should have forgave him, not just for you but for
us"

He had wanted to say more but couldn't find the words
And so for a second the only sound was the birds
From outside the window singing their sweet songs
For a bird life is simple with no sense of right or wrong

She cried
Maya cried more tears than a monsoon
"I wish I could forgive you, but I never can
I'll never betray my father for any man
My hate must overpower my love, I know you most of
all understands"

For was she not forced to make a similar choice he had?
The choice of their love or revenge for her dad
And if he didn't pick their love than why should she
listen?
Why does the woman always have to make the
concession?

Confused
Maya had never felt so confused

It overwhelmed her fear of the situation
Still for Jalal she had to awaken
But it felt like there was no way of escaping

Her country said they did not 'negotiate with terrorists'
And so there really was no leverage
That she could use to help her escape
She knew all she could do now was wait

It's fate
'It's fate' thought Pablo 'It must be'
Although he had absolutely no idea why
He lay on his back looking up at the sky
And knew he had the fate of his love to decide

For with no use they would have to be killed
Otherwise it would make future threats not seem real
But how could he kill Maya and her son
Pablo felt lost not knowing what was to be done

Escape
He decided to help her escape
And with Maya's family he fled
Knowing if his comrades caught him he was dead
But he still had hope despite what she had said

For an impossible dream is better than none at all
And he was ready to climb even an infinite wall
For he had no other hope of happiness in this duniya
And despite the period of time he could only love her

The Plan
The plan was simple but dangerous

He told the guard at the cell that he had received word
That the prisoners were to be transferred
Once he led them out they took flight like a bird

They ran as fast as could not looking back
Fearing at any second they could be under attack
At the port Pablo had arranged for a boat to be waiting
And to Mayas home nation it did take them

Afloat
Afloat Pablo stayed in his cabin
Apart from the captain he spoke to no one
Trying to figure out now how could he go on
After seeing Maya it only made him more lonesome

For having a window in your cell must be a curse
Seeing birds flying free must make incarceration worse
Seeing what you long for but are unable to attain
To want is to suffer and he did suffer in pain

Alone
Surrounded with her family Maya felt alone
None of them would understand what she was feeling
The man had killed her dad why was she grieving?
And dreaming of someone but your husband isn't that
cheating?

So she wondered was there any way out of this situation?
And she pondered this all the way back to her nation
But this story was filled with so many tragedies
She stayed silent for how could she explain to her
family?

The wind
The wind blew on the top deck
As Pablo came up for the first time in days
And whilst he was staring out at the waves
He knew that he would suffer like this for always

Then beside him on the deck Maya came
She stood silent and then she started saying:
"I don't hate you and I do love you,
But you understand I must still put my father above you"

Please don't
"Please don't, please do this for me
I can't erase the past, but we can make a future together
And there is no way that I can ever forget yeh
I will never betray you, I swear it never"

But he regretted saying that last part knowing what
Was the response that she was about to drop
She looked at him in his eyes without batting a lid
And then she said quietly "You already did"

Back Home
Back home the four of them came
And now that they had safely returned
The fire for Maya in his heart still burned
So towards the woman he loved he turned

His face was full of fear for he knew
That it was an impossible task he was going to try and do
And she could tell with horror by looking at his face
Exactly what was about to take place

"My Love
My love for you is so strong
Sixteen years and it never died"
"And neither has mine" Maya replied
"But nothing's changed" she added with tears in her eyes

For even though he had saved her sons life
It still did not erase what he had done that night
In the alleyway when he shattered her world in two
When he caused her to drown in depressions chaotic
whirlpool

He Knew
He knew now what he must do
Whilst standing there in the warm night
There was only one way he could make things right
He couldn't stand to leave her once more and take flight

For he knew now things could never go back
To how they were before he committed that fatal attack
All that was left now was to give her justice
For helping her even if she hated him is what love is

A Blade
He gave her his blade saying "Take revenge"
She still loved him far more than life
Far more than the man who called her wife
But for her father's sake she stabbed him with the knife

As the pain shot through Pablo he still managed a smile
Knowing a greater pain he had felt for years would be
gone in while

Part of him had hoped she wouldn't be able to do it
But after what he had done she had to and he knew it

Hopeless
Hopeless was how she now felt
Despite all that happened those years before they did
depart
She had always clung onto a piece of hope within her
heart
But now that hope was gone the endless tears did start

She had made her decision and she didn't regret it
For the past was too much that she couldn't forget it
She knew that finally her father had been avenged
But why was it his daughter who had to suffer the
consequence

No More
She could not bear to go on no more
Chad took Jalal knowing how this would finish
And didn't want his son to see what he had envisaged
As Maya took the knife and stabbed herself with it

She felt a burning and then she saw
That Pablo was still breathing bleeding on the floor
She looked in his eyes and saw he was shocked
She hadn't wanted him to know the second part of her
plot

"But Why?"
"But why?" was all he could say
"Because a life without you I can no longer live"
She leaned forward and kissed him on the lips

And though they were dying they both felt bliss

For that kiss, Pablo felt his decision had been worth it
And now he could die having completed his purpose
And Maya too felt happiness at the end of her life
For she had avenged her father and rekindled her love at
the same time

A Bench
On a bench, they lay together
Their traumatic history even love couldn't mend
And so in the park they met this is how the story ends
As it had started all those years ago: on a bench

See hate breeds hate in a vicious cycle
Yet for a moment of hope it seemed love might shine
through,
And break the chain that hatred had created
As love is an emotion which is so sacred
For love can create life and build unity
Whilst hate can destroy even whole communities
And Allah will say on that final day:
"Where are those who love each other for My glories
sake
I will shelter them in My shade on this date
Today there is no shade but only My shade"[22],

So first of all love Al-Wadud[23]
For the Most Loving will always return your love

[22] Source: Ṣaḥīḥ Muslim 2566 (A book of Hadeeth)

[23] One of the 99 names of God in Islam, in English it translates into: The Most Loving

How can one live without love and devotion?
Whilst hate is such an illogical emotion
Shaytan hates you so much that he's willing
To burn for eternity just so you can burn with him
So follow the example of how our prophet was living
And if a man wrongs you be ready to forgive him
But for Pablo his hate was just too strong
And he made a decision despite knowing it wrong,
As hate is a tool used by the accursed
And for Pablo his hatred kept on getting worse
It led to murder and ended in suicide
Whilst it is an awful sin to end the gift of your life
You can't ask for God's forgiveness after you've died
And when His judgement comes there'll be nowhere to hide
So Pablo was the biggest victim of his own hate
Which ultimately led to his awful fate,
Yet knowing this couldn't fight his loyalty for revenge
Oh what a tragic story, the story of a bench

Iqra Publishing ©

You can find out more about Hüseyin Abudharr Ali at

www.huseyinabudharrali.wordpress.com

Or follow him on social media at

www.facebook.com/officialrebelfrenzee/
www.twitter.com/huseyinalikosti
www.instagram.com/huseyin_abudharr_ali_diakides/

Cover image is North Muskham in Nottinghamshire.
I would like to express my eternal gratitude towards Dawn Gobourne
and Douglas Williams for their help in promoting this book and to all
my amazing friends who took time to read my poetry and give me
advice, support and encouragement. Also to my parents and my
sister for their support and encouragement. May Allah reward you
all. Lastly, I would like to thank Allah Himself, who has no partners.
No one has the right to be worshipped but Him.

48681574R00049

Printed in Poland
by Amazon Fulfillment
Poland Sp. z o.o., Wrocław